Biographies and acknowledgemen

Ainsley Cocks was born in Redruth and grew up in Par and is a former pupil of Tywardreath school. Fascinated by the mining heritage that surrounded him since childhood, Ainsley took an MSc in Industrial Archaeology at Cornwall College, Camborne before joining what was then the Cornwall Archaeology Unit (now Cornwall Council Historic Environment) in 2001 as part of the Cornish Mining World Heritage Site Bid team. A talented photographer, he is now the Research and Information Officer for the Cornish Mining World Heritage Site, and has travelled the world recording the Cornish mining influence overseas. He is editor of Cornish Mining, the quarterly WHS newsletter.

Steve Colwill was born in Redruth and grew up at the family home in Par where he attended the local school at Biscovey. Much of his young life was spent exploring the old mining remains of Par and St Blazey. From an old North Cornwall family, Steve grew up with a passion for Cornish history and has worked as a photographer, historical researcher and genealogist. Now based in Truro, he is perhaps best known for his in-depth knowledge of early Cornish photography and has one of the largest private collections of early images of Cornwall, most recently contributing to historical studies of Lostwithiel, St Michael's Mount as well as supplying many archive photographs for both publication and broadcast.

This book has come abc supported generously ar .... y a number of people. I am especially grateful to the FEAST Programme for its generous financial support and encouragement. Thanks are also due to Dave and Melinda Ricketts at Creative Edge, Truro for their unfailing friendship, generosity and flair; to Dave Greet at DMG Print; to Karen Willows, who energised the three of us to bring our work together; to James Staughton at St Austell Brewery – a brilliant Cornishman; to Ivor Bowditch for his great knowledge and his struggles on behalf of the china clay industry; to Imerys for its generous community grant; to all those who subscribed; to Reen Barnes and Beth Barker, who encouraged Par Old Cornwall Society to take these poems to their heart; to Steven Wicks – my English teacher at Truro School, who instilled in me a love of the writing craft; to Pol Hodge, friend, poet and massive energy force. Also, the proprietors of the 'Welcome Home' for the use of their evocative pub sign. There is a debt beyond words to my wife, Sue, and our children, who tolerate long silences whilst composing and brewing, and loud hours of rehearsal and composing.

This book is dedicated to the memory of John Barker, who first showed me the Par he loved, and helped me to understand the importance of ports – especially Par and Truro!

It is also dedicated to the memory of Laura Hardman.

Contents

Wheal Martyn

In the hearts of yews at Tywardreath, where echoes
of lost ships slip in Autumn between the solemn bell
and an insistent breeze, Bodrugans and Carminows
whisper of old and new, knotted, twisted in the steps
of the old dance ... and the wheel turns – industry
and profit lie cold as ivy claws its way – a damp aired
song clings about the weed above the door…

Photograph in a Museum Cafe

We, munching faces, the heritage hungry,
We don't look up. We tear into meat
As if the hunt was ours. On the walls
Yelland. Borlase. Hodge. Trethewey –
White-crusted photograph eyes,
Smile from the past with a content
Born of hard-won Redemption.
Their eyes don't blink, nor necks recoil
At the cannon-thunder of Preacher's fist
Crashed on pulpit timbers, his voice
The foghorn in an eternal rock-toothed treachery
Of Damnation's northern shore;
Thick shovel-numbed fingers clasped
Still in Sunday-best-'nd-bowler'd laps.
We pull at salad, reach for drink,
Carelessly clamp burgers in buns, our jaws
Close like death upon sad souls. They,
Behind the hissing, glistening counter,
Stare tolerantly, white crusted eyes creased
In an 'all-the-time-in-the-World' smile. They look
Afraid, behind their eyes, too proud to show –
They worry at the sin of being not unwilling
To dare allow manufacture of their craven image –
The scold! The shrill, wifely threat of damnation
At their Sabbath table, round dough-muscled arms
Draw children tightly into thick skirts. Curiosity

Seduced fear. It's chance, a gamble with God,
To sin, not blink and sit still, the explosion

Whiter and hotter than imagined Hell – and,
Beyond their span, lead letters
Weathered smooth on slight stones.
They will look out from books,
From postcards and museum displays –
Tokens, symbols, imagination-makers,
Fathers of crushing and endless toil.

Temptation!

Easterlies! Bitter morning!
The ocean, ice-smooth, silver,
Spread like glass as far as an eye
Dares to peer, from Par to France.
 Bitter morning! Siberian echoes
Haunt the wake of indolent crows.
The Cap'n's bowler'd shadow
Falls (hopefully) across other drags.
A thin smoke of a crib-hut fire,
Nursed and blown upon, hangs
Like a last breath, over the flue.
Those closest flex cramped feet,
Gaiters creak and argue with crackling furze.
Voices turn and turn old jokes,
And speak of things seen and not seen;
They hang their few words
In the damp-smoke air. To think!
Such shoulders, such arms
Hung in rough-clothed sleeves,
Hands as broad as dinner plates,
Fingers as stout as the plain truths
Of a dark-coated Wesley man, mined
For the clay to make figurines
To warm the jet and opal eyes of mistresses,
And for tinkling cups about which
Seductive pinkie fingers wrapped -
Serpents about an apple's trunk!
Bitter morning! Easterly eyes water!

We dare not forget their names

In the lichen-hung graveyards of peeling chapels lie
Once glorious walrus moustaches, clay-grey,
Brushed down over proud unkissable mouths.
Torn notices half-pinned flutter in the slip
Of speeding, careless cars; boards in window-holes
Like pennies upon departed eyes,
Keep wind and rain from mould-draped pews.

A melancholy voyeur, in search of a mood,
Of injustice to fire an indulgent crusade,
In the charity shop flicks open a book!
Their photograph – moustaches ranged
Beneath bowlers and caps, thick jackets
Buttoned tight in the dignity of Office,
The compassion of firm command their gift -
Clay Captains, long gone-on, stare out.
Their moustaches, groomed for the camera
(No doubt!), intensify the calm which they claimed
From certainty in diligent exercise of duty
And firm belief in the rightness of the Word.

Here, in the valley of books, their gaze is
Of long-passed miners doing the only thing
They knew (before the witness of God) how to do,
In the only land they knew or wished to know,
For the right to bring bread to their children,
For the right to be eternally redeemed – and now,
As we brush past in our purring cars, in our lives,
We dare not, dare not forget their names.

Nature & Man

In the trenches, between slaughters,
Nothing better to do, young eyes
Watched the wheeled horse –
Peerless! *'The working man's truck'.*
Out of sight of Generals (easily done
For Generals were rarely seen!)
Boys whistled between terrified teeth
And dreamed: *'If only we get through*
And back home and all's well
Then Peerless'll be our wagon
And peerless shall we be!'
In the fleet moment between
Armistice and Wall Street
Peerless ran Cornish clay roads
As much as it carried 'Dustbowl Refugees'
Or materials to the Grand Coulee dam.
Now, Shall I compare you, Peerless,
Under shellfire at Passchedaele –
Yon driver hunched through Hell
(something worse than Hell, some say!)
Compare you then, Peerless,
To the barrow of a 'Kettle Boy' -
Till Jarrow emptied and prices fell:-
Compare you to the mighty Foden
That bears the white mountain
Out of the pit day after crawlered day?

Ah! Peerless! You were like the Spriggan
Lightly rolled across the heather,
A machine moved by reason, by purpose
To be the placer of bread on plain tables
In small kitchens, where God sat down to eat,
And the heather spread out its purple mat
From the window to the pit.

The Fear

"The sand drag is clean.
I call to mind the Preacher;
Oh! The thrill of Revival!
The taste of meat is better
When cooked upon the bone
Of faith renewed each Sabbath
And tested before the flood
Of weekdays wash from the pit.
'You've shawn yer fit for'un!'
Redemption drives me on,
The thought of it, the joy!
Then, that damning finger!
The pulpit afire! The Minister's
Shaft to my heart. Our first words
For days; first real words, I guess,
Since our vows stuttered between us -
 I told her, 'cross the table one evening,
'Even though my body hurts,
My thoughts are slow as a water-wheel
And my hope as dull as pig-iron
I wake at night wet,
As wet as a pit in full production –
No matter revival, forget the hymns,
It's the fear of it, of Forever,
For longer than the clay will wash,

For longer than my stone will stand,
For longer than time itself. Tell me .Lover!
Tell me of a safe shore, of grace, of 'home'!"

The tenacity of life

We leave our shirts and shoes
And wander in the heat. Dark as a blade
Combat tempered, the cormorant
Methodically quarters the sea and dives.
Below its green and brown tidal spew of weed
A sweet ocean drizzles and runnels ashore,
An innocent lullaby on crystal lips.
We've had months of rain. Even the granite
Is sodden! The blue sky this morning
Raised uncertain, unexpected thoughts.
'Why!' She said. *'If we were less urbane*
Wouldn't we clasp our hands, fall on knees
And call out for the harvest, for wheat
And barley, and plead for the rotting hooves
Of doleful cattle in the valley, dry of milk?'
A bent thorn, crafted by centuries' gales,
Blind and relentless in its deep grip of the soil,
Tight as a blind man's hand on a guiding arm,
Dark-suited, tight-leaved, tightly buttoned –
The thorn is like the Word itself, firm
In the glare of the sun, unyielding to the anger
Of the wind, taut in its mission, a plunged dorsal
Silhouetted starkly against blue skies, a cleaver
Through the weak flesh of sinful rejoicing! The Word
Stuck like a fishbone in its narrow, tap-root throat.
The thorn bends before the lash of the gale
And stands still in the heat of newly naked sun –
With orchid seed and spider, it will not give way.

Waiting for closure

In the shadows
Between buildings
Where soon
No body will go
To carry this
Or that over there,
To nip off for a fag
Or hide for an hour
To calm feelings
Before something
Best unsaid
Bursts out and blows
Up – spiders itch
To get going
At their weaving
And sequestrations

Such a Storm!

The mistress of light, seductress of sight,
Ripener of apple, tightener of flesh
Over well-moulded bone; over there,
In the flat mirror of a placid sea,
Reddens her lips, plucks brows
And curls her lashes to flutter
At chariots passing and roses of red.

Shimmer in her passion. Across the horizon
Pass ships. Translucent, they deceive the eye;
The desert's trick of mirage teases
Like a rival, ravenous mistress -
It has them merge and emerge, a shadow game!
They ply the ancient lanes, laden low,
Between continents, between languages,
Between defences, between beauties.

And there lies France! In her Board Room
Gallic hands flick croissant crumbs
Across the bottom line, tap their papers
And turn to the business of strangling Par.
Oh! Just across this gentle glass
The mistress of light dabs a finishing touch
To herself, her work of art.
Par, a silent wife, moves about her kitchen.
Such a storm brews, deep in her hold,
Deep in her belly, beyond justice's bells -
Such a storm!

Gathering echoes

Upon Par Sands. Witness!
Marram and sea-rose anchor
These shallow dunes. Stand!
The fields of Trill above Little Hell,
The Gribben calls the unshaven to task:
(Gulls drown the slap of blade on strop
In the shop along the Green
before the 'Welcome Home!') Stand!
Look at the quays and the dries of Par –
Steam shafts, earnest brimstone prayers,
Gush up to wash the underbelly
Of thickly corrugated clouds. Hear this song!
    'Oh! What will become of Par
    When the French have upped and gone?'

If sailors don't dock, and holds don't fill,
Par's sweet girls'll find no venture
In the overtures of boys they shared with school!
Bloodless behind pinched tight lips,
Their laughter too loud, too false,
Their eyes will grow too dull
To be looking about for ships.
When the kaolin air is pungent with sunblock,
And the eye can see from Polmear to Spit –
A gift of the demolisher's sudden art – Then, hear this song!
    'Oh! What will become of Par
    When the French have upped and gone?'

Ground gears of labouring trucks speed clay
To potteries and mills. In the days of pretence,
Between knowing a thing's to be done
And the moment of its doing (between 'Amen!'
And the switch of the plunging, revolutionary blade)
Echoes gather – old voices, quiet through the years
Of industry and profits spent – they call from the hearts
Of tall Tywardreath yews planted to shelter the dead.

From superstiticious ages, Bodrugans and Carminows
Whisper of turning wheels, of old and new
Knotting and twisting in the steps of the dance.
In the damp air hangs the words of a song:
    'Oh! What'll become of Par
    When the Frenchies have upped and gone?
    Will we stand upon these broken quays
    To watch the setting sun?
    Have pity on the stevedore
    With no cargo to upload?
    Be sad, be sad for the sailor without ship
    And for the Mate with no sailor to goad:
    O! What'll become of Par?

On Helman Tor

i.

Only the stiff wood and tight leaves
Of thorn harmonise with the gorse –
I pass between them; they tear my skin.
The wind tugs at my spirit to hurry.
There are no voices and no ghosts.
The wind about my ears
A relentless melody – its pitch
Cuts like wire; whistles like pain.

ii.

Buzzard the Eye
Buzzard the Claw
Buzzard the Ripping Beak
Circle in trinity over the gorse.
The sinner shrew,
For better, for worse,
Scurries at noon
Out of the shadows –
And the Buzzards,
Three, of Helman Tor,
Harried by larks,
Circle the sun and soar.
The sinner shrew
Beneath the fern
Repents in confession
Heard by Lark, a priest,
And thanks the shrew god
For such luck! Below,
At Gunwen, Bryant's door,
Thick stoical chapel oak,
Slams hard, shuts fast,
Shuts out forgiveness.

iii.

Dismembered granite tongues loll,
Cut out of seismic mouths
During geologic torture of the land
And its molten beasts.
Ancient runes and lizard gossips
Hang still in the stiff lacework
Of the thorn – the cricket tuts
And clatters leg-rubbed disapproval;
In the sun, gorse clicks and stutters,
Dry, combustible - the golden crone,
Watches all. These granite tongues
Say nothing; wise stones!

iv.

Each man spreads out his cultivation
From his house. One turns wet hay
To catch the uncertain sun;
One walks uneasy amongst faltering calves;
One lays out square fields,
Another follows his eye; their neighbour
Allows scrub oak to colonise.
On Helman Tor the buzzard's cry
Hangs in every shadow – and the fight,
The struggle without end, carves out holdings,
Marks territories – tractor and hawk converse
Across the first still day of summer.

July 29th 2007

And thus we age, you and I

It's morning. I look over a flat
Reflective sea, towards other lands.
Thirsty, the returning sun
Sucks dew from the benches.
At noon, with shading hand,
I stand and squint
Through its cloud-scalding climax.
I trace the hand of farmers
Along furrows, along ridges of silage
Turned and turned to dry -
Between hedges, in old lanes,
The chug of tractor,
The bellow of cow – dark looming hills!

Then down again, towards evening,
Red and orange, hissing flame,
Dark spotted, the spent sun plunges
Into the lake, slaps the backs
Of startled silver fishes – an egret,
Elegant as a moral question,
Plucks out, with a surgeon's finesse,
A blanched and careless sprat.

The hands, the long and the short,
Climb easily their numbered, moonlit face;
The evening's mountain claimed,
Their midnight summit a chime. Heavily
Hooded, each shadow watched,
From stalking prey, suspicious, to the kill,
Red-rimmed, night-tortured eyes
Retreat. Only, as we sleep, does the wheel
Turn beneath the weight of measured water,
Spoke by spoke – and thus we age, you and I.

Salmon Fishery

For twenty minutes say the rules
These three may lay their net
For salmon that pass between
Polruan and Fowey, and down to the sea.

They sit, stones worn to their rumps;
Too long sat under juniper and ash.
Black thigh boots and scale-stiff aprons
Accent the paleness of their faces.

The tripper-boat-skipper
Says his piece – on tradition:
'They don't seem able t'let'un gaw!'
On price: *'A fresh salmon'll fetch a bob or two!'*

They sit still, fishermen, impassive,
Their stillness the spring of their trap.
Their thoughts, spread like swaying nets,
Are maybe of angels, maybe of a pint!

Our engines throb through the water;
I look into their small faces, and try to see
What laughter lies, what anger, behind salt skin;
I try to absorb their passion for waiting!

The eyes, dark and resigned,
Know too well the salmon – that the salmon
Seem to know the rules set the odds against men!
'What creatures!' If salmon could think!

I want to ask their eyes why they come,
Why set such rules, why sit, and return
To sit again. I guess that they talk, mutter:
'Bleddy trippers; bleddy bawts!'

What's to become of Par?

i

It looks from here, Polpey,
As if Polmear Hill slides up
Like a grey serpent
To meet the early sun -
To speak with it, perhaps,
To tempt or to offer
Some Hippocratic counsel;
As if the sun should know
The consequence of shedding light
Into the untidy corners
And brambled lanes of Par.
The sun is as wise as any star!
Its planets know this
And loyally orbit –

None more so than teeming Earth.
Earth! Where the tendrils of heat
And suckers of light
Crawl fluidly from day to night to day
In their millennial habit.
So, the Sun will have little to do
With the hissing of snakes,
And Polmear Hill lies still
As the milk lorry crawls,
Up, changing down, to be
In Lostwithiel before the paper-train.
Par Dries offers reflection
To the old Sun's caress –
It flumes white funnels
Upward through windless dawns –

Steam fingers, as sternly straight
As Admonishment for misdemeanours
Handed down on Mondays
From the hard Bench of Truro Court.

ii
Since the Quaker Cookworthy (a good man –
No worthier clay-baker could've been!)
Painted his name on a Plymouth mug
And raised the shout for porcelain;
Till even old Wedgewood heard
And come running to examine the fuss;
And Treffry from over t'Fowey
Laid tracks for carrying lime
Through Luxulyan's valley
From Newquay to the main line,
The port of Par has been a white harbour
(or slightly yellow unless
Old Cap'n Pengelly give'd orders
For the subtle addition of bluein'!)!
Par Dries has bellowed
Silent steam and sent trucks,
As regular as passing time,
Out along the company road
Between the Sands and the Green –
Trucks which measure

Upheaval and extraction,
Which defend the pits,
Put food on tables, and clothes
On children, and chalk on the board.
Prayers, spoke clearly out
From pitch pine pews,
With fingers pointed from pulpits
In Trethosa and Trewoon and St Blazey,
as hard as Truro magistrates, only worse
For administering God's law,
Give thanks for a good price fetched!

iii
Shall these stacks go cold?
Shall ships not glide, low in the water,
Out of this white harbour?
Shall grass and rust creep over these roofs?
Or, the spirit-raising shouts
Of Polglase and Yelland not echo
From Littlejohn's and Hendra
To the flat poppy fields of France?
Shall the 'Welcome Home'
Slam shut its door, the paint
Flake from its sentimental sign?
As sure as the scythe
Strikes at the stem, or the box

Is laid in the earth, or the strains
Of *'Abide with Me'* fade
In black-scarved kitchens,
Men will descend with theodolite
And pen and artists' impressions,
And offers in long envelopes
Marked: *'Refusal Not Advised'!*
Crude despots in distant Board Rooms
Will order the cutting-out of miners' tongues
To silence the howls of shovels;
Their pinstriped ants, with plans rolled
Like treaties to unfurl and sweep
Generously with manicured fingers,
Will rush importantly about!
Old miners who *'see'd it all cummin''*
Will sit at tables with their pint
In the *'Welcome Home'*, exchanging glances,
Lending coins for Frank Sinatra
To do it again in the juke-box, and the rust
And the grass will spread like carpets.
Thin, glassy waves, jealous lips,
Will pearl ashore, spewing lighters, condoms
And black crackling weed to cover the echoes
Of stevedores' jokes as they fade along the tide-line.
And from here, Polpey, as the sun spits up
And closure's cloak wraps tightly about

The windpipe and larynx of Par; as I,
Armchair'd poet, plunge my writing hand
Into dark weed and thick water –
As I scrawl metaphorical amusement
And assumed anguish for a place
I know more by reputation and romance
Than by being there, by breathing the white,
Dusty air, running for chips, knocking out
Garden walls for parking – I make my marks
On white, smooth paper, my ball rolls easy
And bold lines ladder down the sheets –
Without thinking, I turn to take another,
Ream on ream, and Par's steam belches
All the while. I sit tight
With Clayman and Docker
And the tide slips over from France.

iv

I stroll in the morning along the Green
In search of a stamp for a card I'll write:
'Dear Reader, I've tasted a morsel
Of the City of Par, set on its counter,
Cut into cubes – Yes! Par!
Where slow fields slide down to the dunes;
Where seeds keep watch with the heron;
Where small houses keep gardens tidy

And white water trickles through leats;
Where the priest waits for appointments
From Bryanites to make Confession!
Where ragwort and marram cling
Like boys to the back of the dustcart;
Where dark eyes turn on the tides
And mark the high sides of long ships;
Where clouds come to fill their cheeks.

v

O! See their pale, uncreased necks,
White as a tern's dropped feather,
The girls, who slip thin scarves
Into the air to wave 'God Speed'
And 'Swift Return!' to their sea-legg'd sailors.
And, here, My Dear, is Par! And, it's coming!
The last ship to stand off,
To wait for Par's last cargo,
Standing off Spit Beach,
Standing off for its Pilot!
And deep in the unseen dimensions
Behind history's brittle curtain,
Tight-buttoned, brilliantined
And lusty voices, a choir of ghosts,
Gently mingle with the wind.
A querulous voice, pulpit trained,

Shaking with excitement
At damnation reversed, redemption
Plucked out of Sabbath skies,
Calls across from Gribben to Black Head:

Oh! Neighbours! Sinners!
Loverin! Pochin! Keay! Boscawen!
Dalton! Sessions! Stocker!
Martin! Nicholls! Bowditch! Selleck!
Oh! What's to become of beautiful Par!
Oh! What is to become of Par?'

August 2007.[1]

---

[1] The Port of Par and one set of Dries closed in
November 2007.

The Sandfly's Mission

The ocean slaps down a disgruntled wave –
In the bar a player throws out his last card –
In black, shrunken lines of weed and wood-sliver,
Of broken boat and tired tree, tides relieve
Themselves of their burden and the beach
From above seems to bear a worried brow.
I disturb the scavenger-rook at supper
And kick through the sand-flies' yard – crisp
The crushing of sun-baked detritus. As I walk
I hope for a treasure, or a curio – cheap perfume
Mixed with oil and salt, after its cross-current ride,
Holds little of the lady who cast it ship-side;
The flintless lighter says nothing of its Third Man
Down by the docks, or his pursuit of spies.
In the bar the dealer flicks around another hand –
The tide turns, imperceptibly, like fear
In the bowel of the refugee at a checkpoint –
Thoughtless me! I've broken the cycle!
The sandfly and the rook are each confused! The ocean
Insinuates a curdling, shoe-drenching wave. Too late
....to run

Par Sands Caravan Park

It would take nothing more
Than walking in, taking the vans,
Declaring intent
For this to become Soweto
Or shanty-town Rio
Or travellers in buses

At United Downs –
The charm of ice-cream bells,
Casual tennis, dogs on leads
Might give way to drums,
All-night fire parties and hooch
In anonymous bottles
Passed from derisive mouth
To evasive mouth.
Perhaps there are enough
Homes to be taken for all
Who call doorways their maisonette,
And take showers from the sky;
And Jack & Alice and loud Dad
Might step aside, take mousey Mum
And go – no harm done; no
Hard feelings. It may not be long
Before beachside suburban illusion
Transforms, and old warriors,
Young runaways, slaves to the needle,
Fools for the bottle, and the plain
Unwanted and unwashed, the broken
Take this place for their own
And erect a sign: *'Welcome
To the township of Hell!'*

National Trust?

O! Recusant Arundels, death-dutied out!
Your gentle Trerice, your cleansed home,
History's clinic, its pale walls yellow
With lichen brittle as old confessions
Urgently whispered - and Calvinists rapping
With swords dripping at this now
Over-greased, conserved great door.
I come for sanctuary, hunted and hungry,
To not vent false proletariat spleen,
but to call on you to take me in. It's said
That Arundels, knowing well sanctuary's breach,
Yet never once failed to close their door
Behind a shivering back, pursued and breathless.
This Time, our Time, famed for tolerance
Of dissent and difference! Mockery's Time,
Scoffs at honour; boils whale-fat loyalty to perfumed
Commodity - Such a Time! Arundels banished
From their prayer-weathered house, this Time
Rummages in the table-tops of history!
Declares itself superior! Enlightened! Rid of 'All That'!
But no! A new Mistress of Trerice, She-Inquisitor!
Head of Sales! Pins me with her eye;
Demands to know why

I seek no more than sanctuary and food; and why
I do not wish to pry behind a sterilised rood.
Escaped, amongst trusting trees, my small prayer
A sand-grain beside *'Hail Marys'* muttered on scaffolds
As collars rolled back on Arundel necks.
"O! Trees! Spread and engulf
These gardens and rooms! Plunge avenging boughs
Through windows! Reclaim this clearing; banish
Coarse words, seductive eyes, the clenched catechism
of 'Product'!" What final humiliation
For the quiet protestation of faith,
This final rack-stretch of mortised joints
And masoned stones which make this recusant place!

Newquay

I'd stood in Newquay Harbour. A scruffer
Shuttled a crabber's catch.
Oilskins and curses
And knackered boys raced for market.
Time pressed. I walked up into town –
The clang and scrape of slot machines -
Clattering hooves of zealous preachers
On the heels of sinfully righteous men!
I thought as I ran
I'd ascended to Babel. I ran and I ran!
In each doorless way
Shadows slid through artificial nights;
Electronic noises passed for gossip.
In a side-street bookshop
Expenditure devoured income
As the Proprietor looked on – blood-sport!
The pale crowd, sun-tanned,
Red-eyed, stares set, men an tol
In slate-dark discs on drawn faces
Unused to light, unused to words.
In Babel the child chews
On the feeding hand; it spits
The gristle of generosity

Into an eye momentarily distracted
And disgustingly beholden to beauty.
As I ran through suburbs hydrangeas
Browned by drought and shrivelled
Fuschia lanterns bobbed; if they could weep
Then tears would meet the tide
Edging through the harbour's gate –
Thus perhaps, for the myth-maker,
May we explain the salt taste of the sea;
That sideways dance of the crab!
But not (Oh Fear!) the vacant lust
For day to be night, night darker, blacker
Than night, strangers' tasteless lips locked tight!

After a Night Tide

Behind Polmear Hill, over the silted quays
And Stannary vaults of Lostwithiel,
The not-so-young Sun dabs on blusher,
Clamps and rolls glistening cherry lips
On a cumulus tissue, and, matter-of-factly
Traces with a thin, manicured finger
The furrows of laughter and anxiety
Which crease from stiff lashes almost
To ring-stretched lobes. On the beach,
Terns wheel over retreating waves.
There's the timeless rubbing of land to sand.
A gull, its black back muscular, its wail
Fit to waken wounded all sedated
To give knackered nurses easy nights,

Skims in low, a Junkers at dawn,
Little fuel, to strafe the railway –
A final, unloading act of war before breakfast
And the dreamless sleep of pilots returned!
Wagtails high-step across the whitening weed
Of the night tide's debauchery - hackney birds!
There's a promise of rain in the air.
Perhaps old Mother Sun will find the heat
To wipe away the grey mat, or perhaps,
In all her painted glory, the fear of a widow
To be judged easy or disloyal by her ghosts
Will make her lie restless behind her curtain.
Cast-up weed dries crisp like lacquered hair,
And sandflies get industriously down to work.

Snake in the Tree

In the brittle light of Dawn
How smooth the ocean appears.
I could walk, as if on glass,
Or skate its opaque ice.
As I stand and reflect
On the sailor's portrait
Of the ocean as mistress

I ask: *'Why would I step
On to the ocean, and where
Would I think I was going?'*
The sea, rolling time after time,
Replies with a sandy whisper,
Reaching between rocks,
Chasing playfully my dry boots.

Don't feed the birds

A white shepherd's effortless
Orchestration of chattering
Disorganised ducks, the swan's
Elastic, italic neck crooks –
A tall Bishop processionally
Strides, measuring time
Against dignity and effect,
Through his cathedral –
It has draped itself within itself
To sleep, elegantly stowed.
The swan unfurls at Dawn, to move
Silent, distant as one with an ear
For ethereal guidance and an eye

On a wayward flock. Only when coaxed
By high-flung bread to step ashore,
To use its height and reptilian reach
In the exercise of a lower, animal law,
Does Bishop Swan appear clumsy,
Thick webbed feet, hidden engines,
Uneasy on sharp stones and sucking mud.
Of course, it is this lapse, ungainly,
Which captures a critical gaze
From the sidelines of Nature
Where cameras and ballpoints click and scrape
And pointing fingers distend mocking minds.

Mrs Gilbert's Date Stamp

"'Ess! 'Ee d'start before dawn,
The pulsin' of trucks up th' Cump'ny Rawd.
Why! A body could measure
Time passing, or a 'eartbeat
By'em! They d'chew tarmac –
In th'awld days, comin' 'nd ' gawin',
Maybe some awld miner
Back from th' Cape might've said:
'They trucks d'thunder
Like wildebeest with a lion
'Ard on their tail!' I dunnaw!"

In small back-land meadows
Ponies bob and chew sweet grass
And swish an odd nipping fly.
Mrs Gilbert unlocks
Her library door. The Estate Agent
And his narrow suit take a stroll
Along Par Green to Costcutter
For milk and his Daily. People
Turn up their A38 noses
Passing through Par – they never
Hear the murmuring conversation
Of the Dries, or listen for a ship's bell
Marking nautical time, counting down
To the tide. And over there,
Over t'John Keay House, sad men

Like priests at the door declaim 'The End' –
Their sandwich board does not, in red letters,
 spell out '**NIGH**'; no *'doom impending'*
That Grandfaithers might've woken
A slumbering congregation with,
Thumping down a believer's hard fist
Upon a pulpit formed
From timbers of salvaged ships –
No! In their corporate helmets
The faceless declare in boardroom
Monotones: *'The port of Par*
Will close; Par Dries will go cold!'

Mrs Gilbert's date-stamp pauses.
The Estate Agent studies the 'market'.
A flotilla of Canada Geese struggle aloft.
A hapless mask, adopted pity,
Like a cataract, films across the Curate's eyes.
The oldest men, forgotten in the corner
Of the Ship, behind their domino walls,
Lost in their euchre school, look up –
They know; they've heard from faithers gone-on
Of the thirties when prices was low,
When pit fought pit, when tables was empty.
Up Costcutter, in the queue, waiting for checkout
And absolution, wives read cards
For small jobs, and worry about their boys

Strolling home from 'waste-of-time' school
And their hands, idle – nothing then
For Par girls to see in *them*. The cards ask
'Who will clear sticks from dead widow's houses;
Who'll paint doors; take down the walls
Of busted gardens, and gravel 'em out for parking?'

In a fading book up Library which Mrs Gilbert
Taps and straightens week after week,
Which never goes out, whose last date
Was stamped in the last century (not that long ago!)
'ee d'say that John Keay – <u>Sir</u> John Keay –
'Ee was a good man – always had time
To stop and hear the choir, gave dinner
To pensioners up Drinnick. He knew
Better 'n most the deadly tie
Between accounts and lines of Bobbies –
Glamorgan coppers, Celtic cousins! –
Shipped in to resist the '13 strike.
Mester Keay (as 'ee was knawn
Til the king gived'un a knighthood! –
Mind, it didn't turn 'is head; not like some!)
He'd seen'em come home;
France was a bitter place, too many pals
Rotting under flat fields. Old Keay,
He made it as right as he could – and now,

There's old Bowditch, the strain
Of the choir ringing in his ears,
Trying like a good Doctor t'ease the pain.

Down Par, it's quiet, like the Western Front.
The TV news lady says: *'Lay-offs expected*
In November'. It's August now. Caravans full.
Mrs Gilbert's busy. Tills are ringing up 'Costcutter'.
The Estate Agent's on the phone, checking *'price'*!
Four months to sip the glass; to take the walk
That was always intended in the shadow of the Dries
And hear the clank of chains, creak of cranes
Along the white quays; guess the languages
Of matelots as sealegs shuffle and call for more.
The time-chewing trucks still rush
With loads for mills along the Company Road;
And Par's on a plate, ready for th'taking,
Another Cornish town on the Agency's list!
Muffled, a ship's bell announces the tide.
Mother and daughter, arm in arm,
Never mind scratches, saying little,
Blackberry in backland fields
Where ponies chew sweet grass
And flick the odd, nipping fly.

Undertaker's Choice

In Par I fail to find a poem.
There hangs over the town
A billow, a pall, a bellow
Of sadness – a stoic's mask
Stretched across the houses;
Their window-eyes stare
Straight ahead, no nose
Peeks around a curtain –
Doors remain stiffly closed.
Not surprising I suppose
If, at a moment's notice,
An easterly may rip down
From Siberia, or Notice-to-Quit
Slip like an autumn leaf
Through a letter box.

Gulls grip the warm ridges
Of working Dries, and shiver
Against the day when steam
May no longer rise. In their
Widow-cries gulls give the air
Of mourners, eager to the wake,
Caught up on the doings
And comings and goings
Of all the living before they
Themselves know themselves,

Or, indeed, have arrived
Or imbibed the half-schooner
Provided in memoriam!
And the town lies, porcelain-
Faced on the table, in pine-
Planks encased – Par wears
Its Sunday suit; is rouged and waxed;
And they come from all around
To pay respects and take the sherry!
It is my shame, to find no poem;
My betrayal to have only come
Now, as the key twists
In Cookworthy's white-dusted door.

The hearse purrs like a diesel cat.
Ribbon flutters from the Bearers' hat.
In the parlour, the Undertaker's choice:
Silence – a gull's cry, the only voice!

The stillness of the heron remains

As thin as reed the heron
Invades with stillness
The place it fills – no shadow
Leans at any hour –
Tells no sundial time –
And time swivels the sun overhead.

Being the question,
Its interrogator lured,
The heron waits and waits,
Stilling the pangs,
Stilling the insistent cries
Of it's precarious nest.

The plunge, like light,
Too fast for the twitcher,
Is deathly, a bolt –
So quick the stillness
Of the heron remains.

Welcome Home[2]

Why! 'Tis I, my Love, after many years at sea
Returned – see, I've brought 'ee a caged bird
From a faraway shore. I've done nought
But dream of you, and dream of snoring
In a warm kitchen on a full stomach, and
Drawing easy across the bed to fold you
Like a dream into my embrace, my grasp!
I'd have it that tomorrow is more like
Yesterday and this day, coming-ashore day,
A step back and a step forward all in one,
And feet as confused as a sailor's legs,
Too long rolling with the swell, at sixes
And sevens. As we stood off, and the Pilot
Pulled on his coat to greet our Cap'n,
I looked into the heart of Par - Gribben
And Black Head like two spread knees,
And the white quays as warm as an oven,
Bathed in the steam of Par Dries; my eyes
Stung with the salt of new tears – I saw
Beach Rose, Campion, Sea Parsley, Ragwort
And stiff Marram bend to the breeze
As if they were waving. I stand below your steps
Gazing up. My knock still hangs on shocked air.
Your eyes acclimatise, I feel you look deep,

You measure the years in my face, days without water
And only hard tack, becalmed and sun-mad
Pinching my belly tight. I feel your questions
And I fear my answers for their effect –
I've been away and a voyager's tales
May not be the cup of tea. I have rolled
Bodelva, Biscovey, Roselyon,
Treesmill, Tywardreath, Pontsmill,
Polkerris, Penpillick, Tregrehan
Like good rum around my tongue –
I have thought of taking your hand
To walk, kicking Par sand, shaded
Eyes towards horizon scan for hand-
Liners flicking hooks of mackerel,
Struggling tails a-glint in the morning sun;
And to wrap my eager arm about you
As the swan uprises, a white serpent
With phoenix wings, its eye eye-to-eye
With ours, and to see a small smile
Play across the lips which now, on your threshold,
Half-parted, are hesitant to laugh or scold.
O! Shall the caged bird sing, my love,
Or shall I let'un gaw and leave this Port of Par?
Leave me in, or else, close gently the door, my Love,
And, at the turn of the tide, on the ring of the bell,
I won't look back. Only the silent bird will weep.

---

[2] The sign of the Welcome Home Inn at Par shows a sailor standing with
a woman looking down from her open door

Farewell to Par

A gate shuts.
The garden? Silent!
Fuschia, hydrangea
Turn to the wall.
Ants scurry across
The hot slate path;
Their Queen wails
For homage. A
Spider curls tight;
The dark heart
Of its deadly web.

Fist-thick ropes
Tighten on capstans.
Rails corrode,
Brown without friction.
Crib-hut and weighbridge
Inhabit shadow.
Sea-winds, nosey
As gulls, scour
Sand-drift corners.
The Pilot sits,
Playing cards -
Idle cutter!

Almost beyond
The naked eye
Translucent coasters
Shimmer along
Indistinct horizons.
The Bay of Biscay,
Land's End, the Scillies,
Grind their dark teeth.
The harbour mouth
Is full of trees, and silts
As fine as porcelain clay.
Seeding docks,
Rigid and rusty
Creak as breeze
Turns to wind
And wind to storm.
Chains on the gate!

Oh! We'll go no more
To dances, love,
Along the garden path;
The village lights are cruel.
And no more
Will bridge-bells ring

Down to engine rooms;
Hearts will skip
Their beats no more;
There'll be no leaving,
No bending hearts,
No waving berets,
No turnings away –
There'll be no more
Leavings from
This pale port of Par!

Harry Patch[3]

Harry Patch went back,
Back to his battleground,
To Passchendale,
To say a prayer for the Germans.
As he looked
Across flat fields,
His trenches politely filled,
A breeze catching his hair,
His eyes, which have watched
One hundred and nine short years
Pass in seasons, closed
For the moment it takes
To say a prayer for the Germans.
His fading voice – *'Tell the children!*
War is the calculated slaughter
Of human beings – for what?'
Harry Patch's voice
Haunts fields of oil and poppy –
It slices with the ease of a bayonet
Through the soft flesh of our resolve.
Come! Say a prayer for the Germans!

---

[3]Harry Patch served with the Duke of Cornwall's Light
Infantry. He was the last known British survivor of
Passchendale. He died aged 111 years old in 2009.